A DVD-based study series
Study Guide

JOHN'S GOSPEL

Wisdom from Ephesus

With Michael Card

A DVD-based study series
Study Guide

JOHN'S GOSPEL

Wisdom from Ephesus

With Michael Card

Eight Lessons for Group Exploration

DISCOVERY HOUSE
PUBLISHERS®

Feeding the Soul with the Word of God

The DayLight Bible Studies are based on programs produced by *Day of Discovery,* a Bible-teaching TV series of RBC Ministries.

© 2010 by Discovery House Publishers

Discovery House Publishers is affiliated with RBC Ministries, Grand Rapids, Michigan.

Requests for permission to quote from this book should be directed to:
Permissions Department
Discovery House Publishers
P.O. Box 3566
Grand Rapids, MI 49501

All Scripture quotations, unless otherwise indicated, are taken from the HOLY BIBLE, NEW INTERNATIONAL VERSION®. NIV®
Copyright © 1973, 1978, 1984 by Biblica, Inc. ™
Used by permission of Zondervan.
All rights reserved worldwide.
www.zondervan.com

Study questions by Andrew Sloan
Interior design by Sherri L. Hoffman
Cover design by Jeremy Culp
Cover photo by istockphoto
The background script on the cover is from Papyrus 66, a nearly complete copy of John's gospel. It is one of the oldest New Testament manuscripts extant. The date of the copy is approximately AD 200.

ISBN: 978-1-57293-492-4

Printed in the United States of America

11 12 13 14 / 10 9 8 7 6 5 4 3 2 1

CONTENTS

Introduction: Writer in Residence   7

SESSION 1
The Place to Begin   9

SESSION 2
"What Are You Looking For?"   17

SESSION 3
A Motif of Misunderstanding   25

SESSION 4
Miracles and Messages   33

SESSION 5
Jesus at Your Feet   41

SESSION 6
The Miracle Behind the Miracle   51

SESSION 7
Journey to Jerusalem   59

SESSION 8
The Faithful Disciple   65

INTRODUCTION

Writer in Residence

What life elements influence a writer as he or she puts words on paper? What helps a writer decide which stories to tell and which to leave out? And do these questions matter when we are talking about a writer who is being led by the Holy Spirit to pen what will become part of the Bible—God's holy Word?

Those kinds of questions pertain to the writings of the apostle John for a couple of reasons. First, we can still visit Ephesus, the place he lived when he wrote the book that bears his name. We can revisit some of the sites where he was when he followed the Holy Spirit's guidance to write the book we call the gospel of John. Although Ephesus is in ruins, we can still see remnants of buildings and parks that existed when John was living there. In addition, we know that John was the latest of the New Testament writers—writing late in the first century and perhaps into the second, a fact that gives us a bit of a closer connection to him.

Songwriter Michael Card has examined the life and the writings of John to look for the many ways those two things correspond. And through the efforts of Michael and the *Day of Discovery* television team, we can follow Michael through the ancient streets and past the ancient ruins of the city where John wrote much of the book that has given us helpful insights into the life and times of our Savior.

Michael Card visited Ephesus—not to review Ephesians, the book Paul wrote to the people and the church at that city—but to seek a new and fresh approach to the stories and the lessons John included when he penned the fourth of the New Testament Gospels while living there.

As Michael reveals, John's book is very different from the first three gospels. This makes us grow curious: What makes it different? What influences led John to write about things that Matthew, Luke, and Mark didn't mention? How did the city influence what John said? You'll benefit from reading the gospel anew and being engaged with it at what Card calls "the level of your imagination."

Walk with Michael through Ephesus and Israel to get a brand-new look at the twenty-one chapters in the book of John.

—Dave Branon
Editor

SESSION 1

The Place to Begin

DAYLIGHT PREVIEW

John's City

When you think about the ancient city of Ephesus, which Bible writer comes to mind? Probably Paul. It was, after all, Paul who wrote the biblical letter that bears the city's name. But Ephesus was also John's city. It was here that the son of Zebedee lived out his long life. In a city that was a center of both trade and pagan religion, John served in the church started by Paul and wrote the New Testament book called The Gospel According to John. It is from this base—far from Jerusalem—that the "beloved disciple" penned his account of the life of Jesus Christ.

COME TOGETHER

Icebreaker Questions

1. The Temple of Artemis in Ephesus was one of the seven wonders of the ancient world. What is the most impressive man-made "wonder" you ever visited?

2. How active was your imagination as a child? Did a parent, teacher, or other adult ever tell you that you had an overactive imagination? Why?

3. Who do you remember for their storytelling ability when you were growing up? Do you know any good storytellers now?

 FINDING DAYLIGHT

Experience the Video

Feel free to jot down Video Notes as you watch the presentation by Michael Card. Use the space below for those notes.

─────────── **VIDEO NOTES** ───────────

Paul and Ephesus

John and Ephesus

Michael Card's introduction

Sister city of Jerusalem

Temple of Artemis

Artemis: The god and the temple

Paul's riot

John: The last living disciple

What we know about John

Jesus' relationship with John

Jesus at John's feet

The unique gospel

WALKING IN THE DAYLIGHT

Discussion Time

---INTRODUCTION---

The apostle John, the longest-living disciple of Jesus, spent the latter part of his life in Ephesus leading the church that was established by the apostle Paul. We will focus much of our attention in this session on the ancient city of Ephesus and Paul's pioneering work there. Ephesus was the capital and leading commercial city of the Roman province of Asia, which comprised a significant section of Asia Minor. Located in modern western Turkey, Ephesus had an estimated population of 250,000, making it one of the largest cities in the world at that time.

In Acts 18:18–21, Luke, the author of Acts, tells us that the apostle Paul briefly visited Ephesus during the latter stage of his second missionary journey. Paul returned to Ephesus during his third missionary journey. Acts 19:1–7 recounts that he immediately met twelve men who considered themselves disciples of Jesus. Their understanding of Jesus, which was incomplete, had evidently come through John the Baptist or some of his followers (see also Acts 18:24–26). Upon their acceptance of Jesus as the focus of their faith, Paul baptized these men.

---DISCOVER GOD'S WORD---

Discussion/Application Questions

1. **Beginning with Acts 19:8, Luke summarizes Paul's time in Ephesus. Read Acts 19:8–10.**

    a. Why do you think Paul followed the pattern, as he did elsewhere, of beginning his ministry in a new city by preaching in the Jewish synagogue?
    - He was starting w/ his own people
    - Likely he was invited b/c of his reputation
    - He was literate in Greek + Hebrew

b. The three-month hearing these Jews gave Paul was actually one of the longest he had in any city. Why do you suppose Paul typically wore out his welcome in synagogues so quickly? *They hated the people that he was preaching toward and they couldn't believe in a "King" that had been crucified.*

2. **We see in verse 9 that Paul moved his operations to the lecture hall of Tyrannus, where he led discussions every day. Chances are this was a school used in the cooler morning hours by a teacher or philosopher named Tyrannus and was then made available to Paul during the afternoon, the hottest time of the day.**

    a. Although Paul was stationed in Ephesus for two years and three months, how was it that Luke could say that "all the Jews and Greeks who lived in the province of Asia heard the word of the Lord" (verse 10)? *He wouldn't have left. People didn't move during that time of day so more could hear.*

    b. What does the fact that Paul stayed in Ephesus longer than in any other location during his missionary journeys say about the importance of Ephesus? *Because it was filled with important people. location, location, location all the sin was found there*

3. **Continue looking at Luke's account of the impact of the good news on Ephesus by reading Acts 19:11–20.**

    Verse 11 appears to refer to direct healings that came through the laying on of Paul's hands, while verse 12 refers to indirect healings that came through the application of Paul's clothing as a tentmaker. The "seven sons of Sceva, a Jewish chief priest" (v. 14) might have been related to the family of the high priest in Jerusalem. It is more likely, though, that Sceva and his sons gave themselves this title in order to impress others with their magical powers. Ephesus was a center for sorcery, evidenced by the fact that scrolls such as those mentioned in verse 19 have been discovered by archaeologists. The scrolls were worth several million dollars by today's standards, not because of the quality of the scrolls themselves but because of the perceived power made available through their secret incantations.

What effect did the events chronicled in these verses have on the people of Ephesus and the surrounding region?

- it would have changed everything about their belief system
- they were jealous of his works and tried to mimic them

4. Luke now turns his focus to the riot that broke out in Ephesus. Read Acts 19:21–34.

Artemis was the Greek name for the Roman goddess Diana, although Artemis as seen by the Ephesians was quite different from Diana. The temple of Artemis was one of the seven wonders of the ancient world. The theater mentioned in verse 29 could seat 25,000 people, making it one of the largest outdoor theaters in the ancient world.

a. What were Demetrius' concerns?

Loosing money & his buisness

b. Why did the people react the way they did? What sentiment united them?

they thought they were standing up for something good not rioting
"Political scheme"

c. Why do you think Paul wanted to speak to the crowd?

to exspose the truth or another point of view and to defend Gaius + aristarchus

JOHN'S GOSPEL

d. Why do you think the Jews wanted Alexander to speak to the crowd? *That they had no part in their money losses.*

e. Why did the fact that Alexander was a Jew stir up the crowd even more? *because they blamed the Jews just as much as the Christians and he was a Jew.*

5. Read the conclusion of this story in Acts 19:35–41.

   The city official referred to here was the chief executive officer of the civic assembly. Although he was not appointed by Rome, he was the liaison between Ephesus and the Roman authorities.

   A meteorite may be the source of the claim he mentioned in verse 35 regarding an image of Artemis that supposedly had fallen from heaven.

   How was the city official able to restore order? *He is the law. He explains how to formally handle the situation and he explained they would be in trouble for rioting.*

6. Now we know more about the city of Ephesus and how a vibrant church began there. This was also where the apostle John lived much of his life.

   What do you think it would have been like to sit at John's feet when he was an old man in Ephesus and listen to him tell stories about Jesus? *very neat*

- perseverance
- following the call of Gods will

DAYLIGHT ON PRAYER

A Time to Share

1. Have you ever tried to do what Michael Card encourages us to do—imagine you are present in a biblical story?

2. What do you hope to gain from looking at portions of the gospel of John from the perspective of the apostle John's eyewitness accounts?

3. Do you have a prayer request to share with the group?

DAYLIGHT AHEAD

Michael Card visits the ruins of a beautiful home owned by wealthy Ephesian citizens—a family that knew Plato and Socrates to be great teachers. But as Card goes on to explain, John knew Jesus to be a great teacher as well. And when John first met Jesus, he asked Him a strange question: "Where are you staying?" Card then reminds us that Jesus gave a remarkable answer—a profound answer that He is still imploring us to do today: "Come and see."

SESSION 2

"What Are You Looking For?"

DAYLIGHT PREVIEW

"Come and See"

Those inviting words of Jesus to the apostle John mark the beginning of their friendship. And they still can affect our lives today when we need guidance, help, and strength. When John first met Jesus, he appears to have been startled by the Teacher's question: "What do you seek?" John's rather odd response: "Where are you staying?" was met by Jesus' kind and comforting words, "Come and see." That invitation is still open to anyone who wants to trust Jesus. He still bids us "Come and see" what He is all about.

COME TOGETHER

Icebreaker Questions

1. Ephesus was a city of scholars and teachers. Who was your favorite teacher in high school or college? Why did that person leave an impression on you?

2. Michael Card notes that John's journey with Jesus began in Galilee but ended in the city of Ephesus. What's the longest, or most interesting, road trip or journey you've ever taken?

3. With an estimated population of 250,000, Ephesus was one of the largest cities in the Roman world. What's the largest city you've ever visited? What do you like or dislike about large cities?

 FINDING DAYLIGHT

Experience the Video

Feel free to jot down Video Notes as you watch the presentation by Michael Card. Use the space below for those notes.

——————————— VIDEO NOTES ———————————

A river in Turkey

Who was this John the Baptist?

Wealthy Ephesian citizen's home

Teachers in Ephesus

John meets Jesus

Jesus' first words

"What are *you* looking for?"

John entering the city

The journey

Michael's journey

The miracle of Jesus' presence

"Come and see"

WALKING IN THE DAYLIGHT

Discussion Time

---DISCOVER GOD'S WORD---

Discussion/Application Questions

1. This session begins with Michael Card explaining why John's listeners in Ephesus wouldn't have considered the rituals of John the Baptist in the Jordan River to be unusual. Read John 1:19–34.

    a. Michael observes that John the Baptist insisted that he was nothing special. Why did he do that?

    Luke 1:17 Because "who" he was wasn't important it was "why" he was there that mean everything. To prepare the people for Jesus. "It was John the baptist but Elyn spirit dwelled in him

    b. Who did John the Baptist understand Jesus to be?

    He knew him to be the messiah, Lamb of God, The light of the world.

2. As you read the next scene from John's gospel, found in John 1:35–42, try to imagine that you were there.

    Verse 35 refers to two of John the Baptist's disciples. We know from verse 40 that Andrew, Peter's brother, was one of the two. From the early days of church history it has been assumed that the other is the apostle John, the author of this gospel.

    a. What does it say about John that he was a disciple of John the Baptist? That he also knew that Jesus was the true messiah Humbled

b. What first drew John's attention to Jesus? John the baptist saying he was the messiah

c. How do you think John the Baptist felt about John and Andrew becoming disciples of Jesus? It pleased him

d. How was Jesus' initial reaction to Andrew and John following after Him different from what would be expected of typical professional teachers, who were always trying to drum up followers? He wanted them to be "faithful" followers, not just followers. He didn't ask anything of them. He only invited

e. How do you think Andrew and John felt about Jesus' reaction? Very excited, honoured, nervous shocked they were very trusting

f. How did Andrew and John feel about Jesus after spending the day with Him? They were eager to introduce others to Jesus as they had no doubt he was the true messiah

3. Michael pointed out in the last session that we can be pretty sure that John, because he lived so long after the death of Jesus, was the youngest of the twelve disciples. What would the ramifications be if that indeed were the case? They would like living in a world of doubt. He would have many stories.

SESSION 2—"What Are You Looking For?" 21

4. As Michael also pointed out in the last session, John and Jesus may have been cousins. How would that have affected their relationship if that were true? *It really means nothing*

5. Michael states that Jesus' first question to John is also His first question to us: "What are you looking for?"

Reflecting on your own life: How would you answer Jesus if He were to ask you that question today?

In John's way, we can't allow our anger to cause us to forget God's love for the sinner his temper is transformed
1 John 4:16-17

DAYLIGHT ON PRAYER

A Time to Share

1. Michael shares that he was only six years old when he realized that Jesus was "asking me into His heart" and began his journey with Jesus. Michael goes on to say, "I don't have a flashy testimony. I can't tell you about some great miracle that happened in my life—except for one, and it's the most important miracle; and that's the miracle of His presence. I can tell you that He's been with me. He's been present in my life, even in the darkest times."

   Do you identify with Michael's journey, or is your journey quite different? How can the others pray for your journey today?

2. Michael also states, "The story of the gospel of John is more than just a story about men walking down ancient roads. It's an intimately deeper journey. It's a journey from isolation to intimacy with God. It's a journey from despair to hope."

   To what extent does that depict your spiritual journey, or at least the desire of your heart—something you would like to "Come and see"? What elements of hope do you need for your life?

3. How can the group support you as you seek to live a Christian life?

DAYLIGHT AHEAD

Session 3 of the series finds Michael Card walking down an old street in Ephesus, reminding us again of the goal of his study: trying to listen to the words of John's gospel in the way his first listeners heard those words. Card stops in the front of a building that was once the third largest library in the world. In Session 3, you'll find out why that makes sense in Ephesus—the city from which John wrote his gospel.

SESSION 3

A Motif of Misunderstanding

DAYLIGHT PREVIEW

The No-Parable Gospel

As Michael Card walks through the ancient city of Ephesus, he points out the characteristics that make John's gospel unique among the first four books of the New Testament. For instance, he explains that there is a motif in the book of John about people who misunderstand Jesus. And there is the concept that alone among the gospel-writers John leaves out the parables of Jesus. Card has an interesting theory behind that fact—one that can challenge us in our efforts to live for Jesus Christ.

---——————COME TOGETHER——————---

Icebreaker Questions

1. This session begins with Michael Card's visit to the Library of Celsus in Ephesus. How much of a "bookworm" were you as a kid?

2. What memories do you have of studying or doing research in a library?

3. Michael notes that the gospel of John is unique among the four gospels. What is one of your unique characteristics? (If this is a hard question for you to answer, maybe the group can help!)

FINDING DAYLIGHT

Experience the Video

Feel free to jot down Video Notes as you watch the presentation by Michael Card. Use the space below for those notes.

---— **VIDEO NOTES** ——---

Library of Celsus 20 yrs after Johns death
3rd largest library
held the scribes of many scholars

City of scholars

Motif of misunderstanding the people didn't understand the things Jesus said.

Nicodemus John 3:3 He was told he needed to be born again.

Woman at the well John 4:10 She doesn't understand what he means

People wanting things from Jesus
they wanted truth, bread

Uniqueness of John's gospel
He purposely left things out b/c it was the last book. He never writes in parables

Why no parables?
the entire life of Jesus was a parable in the book of John

Jesus and the woman
Rabbi wasn't supposed to speak to woman
He was offering her the water of life.

Jesus and the disciples
they were all treated differently

Philip and Nathanael: "Come and see"
"Jesus says "follow me"
John 1:46

Nathanael meets Jesus
He was very skeptical
Jesus "saw him under the fig tree."
this ignited faith

The fig tree
Jesus told him that he saw him. Nathaneal knew what he was praying at the time (br the messiah) so he knew it was vealy him.

WALKING IN THE DAYLIGHT

Discussion Time

DISCOVER GOD'S WORD
Discussion/Application Questions
---

1. Michael Card observes that a "motif of misunderstanding" was quite common in John's gospel. The first example he provides comes from Jesus' conversation with Nicodemus, a member of the prestigious Sanhedrin, the 71-member high court of the Jews. Read John 3:1–4.

   a. Why do you think Nicodemus came to Jesus at night?

   because he was afraid of what his peers would think of him. Also could have been out of protection

   b. How did Jesus completely pull the rug out from under Nicodemus' spiritual life?

   Because he was taking the "born again" literally; not understanding it was a spiritual rebirth.

2. Read Jesus' reply to Nicodemus in John 3:5–8.

   There are various interpretations of what Jesus meant by being "born of water and the Spirit" (v. 5). Nevertheless, what was the essence of Jesus' message to Nicodemus?

   He meant being cleansed by the holy spirit and by being reborn spiritually.

3. The next example of a "motif of misunderstanding" that Michael provides comes from Jesus' conversation with the woman at the well. Read John 4:1–4.

   The Samaritans were a mixed race that originated with the intermarriage of Israelites and Gentiles. The Israelites had been left behind when Assyria conquered the northern kingdom in 722 BC and carried many of its people into exile. The Gentiles were brought into the land by the Assyrians (see 2 Kings 17:24). Because of the hostility between Jews and Samaritans in Jesus' day, many Jews avoided Samaria altogether by crossing the Jordan and traveling on the east side of the river.

   When John comments that Jesus "had to go through Samaria" (v. 4), do you think he means this simply due to geography (i.e., because it was the direct route between Judea and Galilee) or because of Jesus' sense of mission? *because Jesus' sense of mission. He could have taken a different way.*

4. Read John 4:5–9 to see how Jesus' conversation with the woman began.

   Jesus arrived at a well named after Jacob, whom both Jews and Samaritans revered as a patriarch of their faith, at noon (the sixth hour). Jesus broke the custom that Jews did not associate with Samaritans. A literal translation of John's parenthetical comment in verse 9 is "Jews do not use dishes Samaritans have used." Jews would become ceremonially unclean if they used a utensil handled by a Samaritan, because they believed Samaritans were "unclean." Jesus also broke the tradition that says Jewish teachers didn't speak publicly with women (see v. 27).

   Why do you think Jesus disregarded these cultural norms?
   because Jesus crossed all barriers to share the good news.

5. **Read John 4:10–15 to see how Jesus' conversation with the woman continues.**

    How is this an instance both of John's "motif of misunderstanding" and of his presentation of Jesus' life as a parable?

    because the woman didn't understand that Jesus wasn't talking about "drinking water." He was talking about "spiritual" water. She thought she would never be physically thirsty again instead of spiritually thirsty.

6. **Read John 4:16–30 to see how Jesus' conversation with the woman concludes.**

    Even though Jesus opens up this woman's life and exposes her sins, how does she end up feeling about Him?

    She wants others to see him. She believes him and tells others it's the messiah. She even leaves her water bucket by the well when she leaves.

7. **Read John 4:39–42 to see what happened after Jesus' conversation with the woman.**

    What was the result of Jesus' conversation with the woman with respect to the people of her town?

    they all believed that he was the Savior of the world.

8. Michael notes that Jesus dealt with His disciples differently. He called John with an open invitation: "Come and see" (John 1:39). But with some disciples, like Philip, He had to be more direct. Read John 1:43–51.

Michael believes that Nathanael was praying for the coming of the Messiah. Others suggest, in light of Jesus' words in verse 51, that Nathanael had been reading of Jacob's dream at Bethel, where he saw a stairway reaching to heaven and upon which angels were ascending and descending (Genesis 28:12). (Note: "Son of Man" was Jesus' favorite title for himself, a title that He clearly considered to be Messianic.) At any rate, Nathanael knew precisely what Jesus was talking about and that he had witnessed a miracle.

What did this experience lead Nathanael to conclude about Jesus' identity? *That he really was the true Messiah*

DAYLIGHT ON PRAYER

A Time to Share

1. What effect should the fact that Jesus knows all about us—as demonstrated by His encounter with Nathanael—have on our lives?

2. Do you think there may be some "motifs of misunderstanding" in your relationship with Jesus—that is, He is trying to communicate to you but you aren't getting it? Are there elements of that situation that need prayer?

3. What prayer requests would you like to share with your group?

Take away - God uses anybody for good for Kingdom expansion Telling about God.

DAYLIGHT AHEAD

Like parties? So did the folks who lived in Ephesus. In fact, some even had pictures of a god of feasting in their homes. Michael Card uses this fact as a lead-in to discuss Jesus and His interest in what was going on at a party in Cana. Leaving that miracle behind, Card then moves to another part of Ephesus to talk about something far different—the mini-sermons found in the book of John. Parties and sermons: two diverse subjects to be explored in Session 4.

SESSION 4

Miracles and Messages

DAYLIGHT PREVIEW

A Party, Some Sermons, and a Serpent

The items John was guided to include in his gospel reflect a long life of ministry and contemplation by the apostle as he lived and served in Ephesus. In an effort to record the story of Jesus as He saw it, he included a rather eclectic group of events: A wedding where Jesus miraculously created wine, a series of sermons that introduced salvation to the people, and an Old Testament story of a serpent on a stake. Yet together these selections join to reveal the Savior in all of His glory—powerful, compassionate, and able to heal people physically and spiritually.

—————— COME TOGETHER ——————

Icebreaker Questions

1. This session begins with the story of Jesus changing water into wine at a wedding feast. What's the most amazing, humorous, or otherwise memorable thing you can remember about a wedding or wedding reception?

2. Who is the "life of the party" in this study group?

3. How do you feel about snakes?

FINDING DAYLIGHT

Experience the Video

Feel free to jot down Video Notes as you watch the presentation by Michael Card. Use the space below for those notes.

———————— **VIDEO NOTES** ————————

Romans and parties

they liked a bit much.

Jesus' first miracle *John 2:1-3 at a wedding party water into wine is a very subdued way.*

John's first hearers

Steak w/ snake wrapped around it.

Homes of the poor

Mini-sermons of John

34 JOHN'S GOSPEL

Son of Man lifted up (Asclepius)

Temple of Serapis
City of cults. This is why John would go there.

The cross: Symbol of suffering
look at your suffering to be healed. we caused this
Ch. 3

The Agora
commercial center where he often preached

The first invitation: "Come and see" *John 1:39*
Jesus said this.

WALKING IN THE DAYLIGHT

Discussion Time

--- DISCOVER GOD'S WORD ---

Discussion/Application Questions

1. We have seen how Jesus, in John 1, met and called some of His first disciples. Now John's travelogue moves to a wedding in Galilee. Read John 2:1–4.

   John's statement that the wedding took place "on the third day" was probably a reference to the third day after Jesus called Philip and Nathanael. The exact location of Cana is unknown, though it was surely near Nazareth, west of the Sea of Galilee. Weddings in Jewish villages like Cana were community celebrations. Providing refreshments, especially wine, for all the guests was quite important. Failing to do so properly would be a social disgrace, a fact that sparked Mary's sense of urgency. Jesus' response to His mother was not as brusque as it seems, for "Woman" was simply a formal expression of address (see also John 4:21; 8:10; 19:26; 20:15).

What do you suppose Mary and those nearby thought Jesus meant when He said, "My time has not yet come"? How was this another case of John's "motif of misunderstanding"?

They wanted him to do a miracle but he didn't look at this simple act as a miracle. They didn't know what he was going to do but they fully trusted him anyway.

2. Now read about Jesus' first miracle in John 2:5–11.

   a. Do you agree with Michael Card that this is "one of those 'unmiraculous' miracles of Jesus"?

   b. What did John see as the greatest significance of this miracle? What effect did it have on him and the other brand-new disciples?

   They all believed. they were able to see his power over nature

3. Michael points out that the Gentiles in Ephesus who later heard John tell this story were steeped in a belief system influenced by the Greek god Dionysus, the god of wine and feasting. Legends associated with Dionysus included stories in which he filled empty kettles with wine.

In light of this reality, how would this miracle affect the people in Ephesus who heard John tell this story? They would learn of the true messiah. That what they had been worshiping wasn't "in the name of Jesus"

4. Michael also notes that the Jewish religious leaders were bothered that Jesus went to parties—and particularly that He seemed to have too much fun when He was there. In fact, they called Him a winebibber. Michael observes, in contrast, that Psalm 104:15 states that God gives people oil to make their faces shine and wine to make their hearts glad.

What lessons about our attitudes toward life and our relationship with Jesus can we take away from this story? That Jesus is Fun! That I want him with me always. Not just in times of need.

5. In Session 1 we considered the first part of Jesus' conversation with Nicodemus in John 3. Now we will take a look at Jesus' concluding words to Nicodemus. Jesus referred to a story found in the Old Testament. About forty years after the exodus from Egypt and after most of the older generation had died, the Israelites were nearing the end of their wandering in the desert. Read Numbers 21:4–7.

   a. What sins were the people guilty of? They were speaking against God.

   b. How did the Lord respond to their sins? He sent out poisonous snakes.

c. How did the people respond to their punishment?

They came to moses and cried out what they had done and asked God to stop.

6. Read Numbers 21:8–9 to see how the story ends.

   a. What was the Lord's prescribed remedy?

   To look at the snake on the pole and be healed. (like looking at Jesus on the cross) to be healed from sin

   b. Was the bronze snake the source of the people's healing? If not, what was?

   no - it was Jesus their belief in God.

7. Now read John 3:9–15 to see how Jesus used this story in his conversation with Nicodemus.

   a. Why would John's listeners in Ephesus immediately connect this story to the god Asclepius?

   b. How did Jesus apply this story to himself?

c. What was the parallel to the story in Numbers in terms of the affliction? In terms of the prescribed remedy? In terms of the cure or result?

DAYLIGHT ON PRAYER

A Time to Share

1. Michael Card states that John lived a crucified life in Ephesus, pouring his life out the way he saw Jesus pour His life out. Do you feel that you are living a "crucified life" where God has placed you?

2. In reference to Jesus' words about His being "lifted up," Michael says, "The cross becomes that symbol of suffering. And we're encouraged to look at that suffering that we caused, and find healing."

   Spend some time in silent prayer, "looking" at Jesus' suffering and thanking Him for the healing, forgiveness, and eternal life that comes as a result.

3. Do you have any prayer concerns to share with your group?

DAYLIGHT AHEAD

The events Michael Card describes in Session 5 all happened in Israel during Jesus' life. But as he walks through the sites of ancient Ephesus, he relates them to John the writer—telling the people of Ephesus about Jesus' miracle of feeding the 5,000, His emotional dispersal of the moneychangers in the temple, and His quiet, humble washing of the disciples' feet. We visit Ephesus to understand better the servant heart of Jesus during His life on earth.

SESSION 5

Jesus at Your Feet

DAYLIGHT PREVIEW

Listening to John's Stories

While we usually think of Jesus' stories such as the feeding of the 5,000, the dispersal of the moneychangers in the temple, and the washing of the disciples' feet in the upper room in terms of their Jerusalem connection, Michael Card offers a different perspective. He suggests that we think of those stories as John told them to his fellow citizens of Ephesus—with the backdrop of that city in mind as the stories are being told. That different approach may help us see these three great stories about Jesus in a fresh new way.

COME TOGETHER

Icebreaker Questions

1. When you were growing up, how often did your mom (or someone else) tell you to "Clean up your plate"? How often have you said that to your children?

2. How do you feel about eating leftovers? Do leftovers ever cause tension in your family?

3. In this session we will look at an occasion when Jesus expressed "righteous anger." In regard to anger, do you have a "short fuse" or a "long fuse"? What percentage of the time would your anger qualify as "righteous"?

 FINDING DAYLIGHT

Experience the Video

Feel free to jot down Video Notes as you watch the presentation by Michael Card. Use the space below for those notes.

——————————————— **VIDEO NOTES** ———————————————

A quick review

Feeding the 5,000

Agora—the marketplace

The story of the feeding

The greater miracle

Temple of Artemis

Changes at the Jewish temple

Jesus would pay the price

Last Supper/footwashing

Jesus and the life of a slave

Jesus at your feet

Michael's wrap-up

 **WALKING IN THE DAYLIGHT**

Discussion Time

---——————— **DISCOVER GOD'S WORD** ———————---
Discussion/Application Questions

1. In this session Michael Card reflects on three key events in the life of Jesus. The first is the feeding of the five thousand—the only miracle of Jesus that is recorded in all four gospels. Read the first part of the story in John 6:1–7.

   Why were large crowds of people following Jesus?

2. Perhaps Jesus posed His question to Philip because Philip was from nearby Bethsaida (see John 1:44). English Bibles vary in their renderings of Philip's response in verse 7. Literally, Philip said that two hundred denarii would not be enough money. A denarius was equivalent to a laborer's average day's wage, so the total amount would have been almost a year's wages.

   How would you have felt about Jesus' question if you were Philip? How would you have likely answered the question?

3. Read about the miracle in this story in John 6:8–13.

   a. Verse 10 states that about five thousand men were present. Counting women and children, there may have been fifteen thousand people. Why would John's listeners in Ephesus not have trouble imagining a meal involving that many people?

b. What does Michael mean that this, like Jesus' changing of the water into wine at Cana, was an "un-miraculous miracle"?

c. Why do you think Jesus told the disciples to gather up the leftovers after everyone had enough to eat?

4. **The disciples gathered enough leftovers to fill twelve baskets—small wicker baskets that Jews always carried with them. Michael reflects that the point here is not abundance but perfect provision.**

    Can you relate to Michael's claim that it's a greater miracle to be *perfectly* provided for—to get just what we need from God—than to have the abundance that people typically desire?

5. **Read how John concludes this story in John 6:14–15.**

    Michael suggests that the people in the back of the huge crowd probably didn't even know that this was a miracle in which Jesus multiplied a meager amount of food in order to feed all of them. John 6:14 reveals, however, that the miraculous nature of the situation eventually became apparent. The people "saw the miraculous sign that Jesus did" and identified Jesus with "the Prophet" Moses had

predicted in Deuteronomy 18:15–18, a Scripture that Jews viewed as a promise of the Messiah.

What kind of Messiah did the people expect, and how did Jesus respond to those expectations?

6. **John records Jesus' cleansing of the temple at the beginning of His ministry, while Matthew, Mark, and Luke have that event at the end of His ministry. Although some scholars believe there was only one cleansing (they say John placed it near the beginning of his gospel for theological reasons), the simpler explanation would be that there were two cleansings—one at the beginning of His ministry and the other at the end. Read John's account in John 2:13–17.**

   Jesus' anger seems to be focused more on where the merchants were conducting their business than upon the business itself. Jews who had traveled long distances needed to be able to buy animals to offer as sacrifices and to exchange their money for currency accepted by the temple authorities for paying the annual temple tax. However, the merchants were operating in the outer court of the temple, the one place where Gentiles were invited to pray and worship.

   John notes, in verse 17, that he and the other disciples "remembered" the words of Psalm 69:9. These words may well have come to them after Jesus' crucifixion (see John 2:22), as they came to see Psalm 69 as a prophecy pertaining to Christ.

   a. How do you suppose the disciples felt about Jesus' actions at the time?

b. How, as Michael points out in regard to John's listeners in Ephesus, was the Jewish temple in Jerusalem becoming what the Temple of Artemis had been for centuries?

7. Michael reflects that beneath Jesus' anger is a deeper level of frustration, a disappointment and hurt that people had come to the place where they believed that salvation and a way to God was something *they* could pay for—because if there's a price to be paid to reconnect with God, if there's a price to be paid for the forgiveness of sins, *Jesus is going to pay it.*

    How much do you think the Lord has that sense of disappointment and hurt in regard to people today?

8. Read about Jesus' conversation with the Jewish religious leaders in John 2:18–22.

    How does this discussion about "this temple" demonstrate another example of the "motif of misunderstanding" commonly found in the gospel of John?

9. Only the gospel of John records the story of Jesus washing His disciples' feet during the Last Supper. Read that account in John 13:1–17.

    a. Why does Michael believe this is one story that John's audience in Ephesus would have had as much trouble understanding as we do?

SESSION 5—Jesus at Your Feet

b. What does Michael mean when he says that Christianity is a slave religion, and that if you don't know Jesus as a slave, John would say you don't really know Him?

DAYLIGHT ON PRAYER

A Time to Share

1. Close your eyes and try to imagine, as Michael encourages us to do, that Jesus is kneeling at your feet. Imagine what it would be like to have Jesus the Savior-Servant, the One who came and lived and died like a slave, kneel before you and wash your feet.

2. Would you like to share anything about your thoughts and feelings during this exercise?

3. One way we can "wash one another's feet" is through caring and praying for one another. Therefore, how can you pray for each other and for those outside the group for whom you carry a concern?

DAYLIGHT AHEAD

Michael Card completes his time in Ephesus by taking us with him to visit two more locations: the baths of Ephesus, where the citizens would gather to relax, talk, and sometimes seek healing; and the main street of Ephesus, where John and Paul would have first walked upon entering the city. At these two locations, Michael shares about two miracles of Jesus—miracles that can teach us more than we usually think we notice about Jesus himself.

SESSION 6

The Miracle Behind the Miracle

 DAYLIGHT PREVIEW

Two Healings

A paralyzed man and a blind man: two citizens of Jerusalem who discovered the healing power of Jesus Christ. Yet the two men reacted differently to their circumstances and to their miraculous transformation. With each healing, Michael Card sees a miracle behind the miracle—which helps us gain new insight into Jesus' pre-crucifixion ministry. The time was coming when Jesus would face the cross, when He would offer healing for all mankind.

--- **COME TOGETHER** ---

Icebreaker Questions

1. This session begins in the ruins of a Roman bath in Ephesus. How often do you enjoy a nice, long, soaking bath or a visit to a hot tub?

2. In this session we will meet a man Michael Card calls "the man of excuses." How good were you at coming up with excuses when you were a kid?

3. In this session we will also meet a man who was born blind. Do you have childhood memories of playing party games blindfolded?

FINDING DAYLIGHT

Experience the Video

Feel free to jot down Video Notes as you watch the presentation by Michael Card. Use the space below for those notes.

———————— **VIDEO NOTES** ————————

Scholastic bath

Three sections

The man of excuses

Harbor pavilion

The man born blind

Miracle behind the miracle

Greeks seeking Jesus

"My soul is troubled now"

Michael's conclusions

WALKING IN THE DAYLIGHT

Discussion Time

DISCOVER GOD'S WORD
Discussion/Application Questions

1. **In this session we will look at two stories about men Jesus healed. Michael Card calls the first man "the man of excuses." Read the first part of his story in John 5:1–7.**

    Most Bible translations indicate with a footnote that some ancient manuscripts of the gospel of John add an expanded conclusion to verse 3 and all of verse 4 (as opposed to including those words in the main text). Be sure to read those words, though, as they were likely added to those manuscripts to explain the stirring of the water in verse 7.

a. How would the ancient idea associating healing with baths influence this perspective?

b. What do you think of Michael's assessment that the man actually didn't want to get well because his disease was really his identity?

c. How common do you think that kind of situation is today?

2. **Read the rest of this story in John 5:8–15.**

   a. How was the man guilty of making a second excuse?

   b. What else about this man, from Michael's perspective, points to a cold heart?

   c. Is it likewise possible for us to cross paths with Jesus, in a sense, and not really come to know Him?

3. **Read John 9:1–5, the first part of the story about another man Jesus healed.**

    a. What assumption about the cause of sickness does the disciples' question display?

    Note: Jesus clearly stated that this man's blindness wasn't caused by anyone's sin. We saw, however, that Jesus said to the man healed at the Pool of Bethesda, "Stop sinning or something worse may happen to you" (John 5:14). Though Jesus rejected the notion that suffering is always caused by sin, He didn't say that suffering is never caused by sin.

    b. How did Jesus view the blind man's affliction as an *opportunity*?

4. **Now read John 9:6–12 to see how Jesus healed the man who been born blind.**

    Jesus could use even the earth's dirt as an instrument of healing. And once again a story of healing involves a pool or bath—this time the Pool of Siloam.

    How did Jesus demonstrate the fact that He is "the light of the world" (v. 5)?

5. **Read John 9:13–34 to see how some Pharisees, members of a legalistic and influential Jewish sect, got involved in the story.**

    Michael notes that he really likes the man who had been blind from birth. What is there to like about him?

6. **Read the conclusion of the story in John 9:35–41.**

   a. How did Jesus demonstrate even more fully that He is "the light of the world" (v. 5)?

   b. How was this second miracle—the "miracle behind the miracle"—even more miraculous than the first miracle?

7. **In John 12:12–19, the apostle John recorded the triumphal entry of Jesus into Jerusalem, an event that took place just a few days before His death. Near the end of this session, Michael reads the passage that immediately follows that account. Reflect on the meaning of John 12:20–28 as a member of your group reads it again.**

   These "Greeks" were probably Greek-speaking Gentiles who, though they hadn't become full proselytes, were attracted to Judaism and had come to Jerusalem for the Passover Feast. They may have approached Philip because of his Greek name.

   Why did the coming of this group of Gentiles with their rather ordinary request rock Jesus?

DAYLIGHT ON PRAYER

A Time to Share

1. John's gospel doesn't include, as do the other three gospels, an account of the Garden of Gethsemane in which Jesus agonized in prayer just prior to His arrest. However, the passage we just considered in John 12 serves as somewhat of an equivalent. In each case Jesus committed himself to obey the Father and go to the cross.

   How does that commitment inspire you to obey the Father and to take up your cross and follow Jesus?

2. How can the group agree with you in prayer in regard to your spiritual life and commitment?

3. What other requests would you like to share with the group?

DAYLIGHT AHEAD

From Ephesus to Jerusalem. That's the transition Michael Card has made as he begins Session 7 of our study. He has made that trip in order to follow the apostle John through the final days of Jesus' walk on earth. After examining John's life and work in Ephesus, Michael now takes a look at some fascinating events during Jesus' ministry where John was intricately involved in what the Savior was doing—the footwashing and the events that lead to Jesus' death. And he examines John's relationship with his outspoken friend Peter.

SESSION 7

Journey to Jerusalem

DAYLIGHT PREVIEW

The Man in the Shadows . . . and His Fiery Friend

We seldom think of how personalities and human tendencies must have affected the lives of the people we read about in the Bible. What kind of a person was John? Was he quiet? Outspoken? And what about Peter? Perhaps we think we know about him because he always seemed to capture the headlines in any situation that arose. Interestingly, these two disciples were close friends—especially at the end of Jesus' earthly life and later. Yet they seemed to be very different in personality. John seemed to be more sedate, "in the shadows," Michael Card says. Peter, well, we know how he stood out. Yet both were men of God who were with Jesus till the very end.

COME TOGETHER

Icebreaker Questions

1. In this session Michael Card makes the point that Jesus loves each one of us as if we were the only one to love. When you were growing up, did your parents tend to favor one child in your family?

2. Do you ever remember being the teacher's pet?

3. In a close relationship with another person, do you tend to be more like the apostle John—quiet and in the shadows—or like the apostle Peter—the one who does most of the talking?

FINDING DAYLIGHT

Experience the Video

Feel free to jot down Video Notes as you watch the presentation by Michael Card. Use the space below for those notes.

———————————— **VIDEO NOTES** ————————————

The Last Supper

John, the beloved disciple

The long, last walk of Jesus

The path to Gethsemane

John and Peter at the gate

Man in the shadows

WALKING IN THE DAYLIGHT

Discussion Time

---DISCOVER GOD'S WORD---

Discussion/Application Questions

1. In Session 5 we looked at the first part of John's account of the Last Supper, in which Jesus showed His disciples "the full extent of his love" (John 13:1) by washing their feet. As we return to that scene, try to imagine that you are the apostle John. Read John 13:18–30.

    a. How would you have felt if you had heard Jesus announce that "one of you is going to betray me" (v. 21)?

    b. How would you have felt if Peter had said to you, "Ask him which one he means" (v. 24)?

    c. How would you have felt after what transpired between Jesus and Judas?

2. **Continue to imagine that you are the apostle John as you read what happened next in John 13:31–38.**

    a. What do you suppose you would have thought about Jesus' words regarding where He was going (vv. 33, 36) at the time He said them?

    b. How would you have understood those words at the time you wrote your gospel?

3. **In John 13:23 we have the first instance in John's gospel in which John referred to himself as "the disciple whom Jesus loved," a description that John would repeat again in 19:26, 20:2, 21:7, and 21:20.**

    a. What would there have been about this experience at the Last Supper that made John see himself this way?

    b. Using Michael Card's terms, what is the difference between a *special* relationship and an *exclusive* relationship?

4. **Michael points out that the bulk of the longest discourse we have from Jesus—John 14–17—took place during Jesus' long walk with His disciples after the Last Supper (see John 14:31) on the way to the Garden of Gethsemane, where He was arrested. And during this long walk Jesus promised the disciples the Holy Spirit. Read John 16:5–15.**

   Why would this promise of the Holy Spirit be, as Michael says, just what the disciples needed to hear?

5. **Imagine again that you are the apostle John as you read about the events in John 18:1–18. (Note: The "other disciple" mentioned in verses 15–16 was likely a reference to John.)**

   a. How would you have felt when Jesus was arrested?

   b. How would you have felt as you followed Jesus after His arrest and then arranged for Peter to be able to join you inside the high priest's courtyard?

6. **Read about Peter's second and third denials of Jesus in John 18:25–27.**

   As Michael points out, while it seems impossible for Peter to stay in the shadows, that's where we find John. Do you think their experience in the high priest's courtyard directly contributed to the fact that John and Peter later were seldom apart?

DAYLIGHT ON PRAYER

A Time to Share

1. Michael Card states, "Jesus loves each one of us as if we were the only ones to love. Beloved disciples are the only kinds of disciples that Jesus has."

    Do you see yourself as "a disciple whom Jesus loves"?

2. How might you nurture and strengthen a loving relationship with Christ?

3. What situations in your life, in the lives of others, or around the world would you like the group to pray about?

DAYLIGHT AHEAD

Session 8 will take you again to Israel as Michael Card visits places both in Jerusalem and near the Sea of Galilee that help him teach more truths about the gospel of John. You join Michael at a traditional spot where some say Jesus' mother Mary is buried, you'll visit a tomb somewhat like the one where Jesus was laid to rest, and you'll see the location where Jesus made breakfast for the disciples. And there's a bonus as Michael picks up his guitar for a special song relating to Jesus' first words to John.

SESSION 8

The Faithful Disciple

DAYLIGHT PREVIEW

Breakfast Club

Imagine coming home from your third-shift job as a fisherman and having someone ask you, "So, what was new down at the lake today?" To which you, "Oh, nothing—except that Jesus fixed us breakfast." How's that for a conversation starter? John had a number of unique privileges as Jesus' beloved friend. Before Jesus prepared breakfast for His friends by the Sea of Galilee, John served the Lord himself by remaining at the foot of the cross and received Jesus' instructions to care for Mary. John was indeed a close, faithful disciple to Jesus when they both walked the streets of Jerusalem.

COME TOGETHER

Icebreaker Questions

1. In this session Michael Card points out that Peter was like a big brother to John. Have you ever had a surrogate big brother or sister? How about a surrogate little brother or sister?

2. John beat Peter in a footrace, of sorts, to Jesus' tomb. Do you recall a time when you were so excited to get someplace that you raced someone to get to the destination?

3. Do you like to fish? If so, what is the best advice someone has given you for improving your success?

FINDING DAYLIGHT

Experience the Video

Feel free to jot down Video Notes as you watch the presentation by Michael Card. Use the space below for those notes.

———————— **VIDEO NOTES** ————————

Three Marys and John

Shadow of the cross

John's friend, Jesus, talks

Herodian tomb

Mary Magdalene runs to Peter and John

John outruns Peter to the tomb

Breakfast by the sea

Why is Jesus there?

One last story

"Come and see"

WALKING IN THE DAYLIGHT

Discussion Time

DISCOVER GOD'S WORD

Discussion/Application Questions

1. This session begins at the traditional site of Mary's tomb in Jerusalem. Michael Card then refers to the story in Scripture where Jesus entrusted His mother to the care of the disciple John. Read John's own account of that poignant scene in John 19:25–27.

Naturally we wonder why Jesus entrusted His mother to John rather than to His half-brothers. Jesus' brother James was probably the oldest of Jesus' brothers, since he's listed first (Matthew 13:55; Mark 6:3). Though James would become the leader of the church in Jerusalem and write the epistle of James, he and his brothers probably weren't present at Jesus' crucifixion and didn't yet believe in Him as Messiah. And some Bible scholars believe that John was Mary's nephew.

   a. What do you think of Michael's belief that Jesus entrusted His mother to John because at this point in his life John needed her just as much as she needed him?

   b. Michael imagines that at the end of Mary's life this man John, who is always in the shadows, was with Mary in the shadow of her death, holding her hand. How is that an image of John as the faithful and beloved disciple of Jesus?

2. **Now read John 20:1–9, John's account of the dramatic events that occurred two days later.**

   a. How does the reaction of Peter and John to Mary Magdalene's words demonstrate, contrary to some skeptics' claims, that Jesus' disciples had no part in secretly removing His body from the tomb?

   b. Why do you suppose Peter immediately entered the tomb although John didn't?

3. Peter and John saw the unusual phenomenon of the grave clothes appearing as if Jesus' body were in them though no body was there. The head cloth was rolled up in a place by itself and still retained the shape of Jesus' head. Had someone taken the body, he would have either removed the grave clothes, leaving them in a heap, or taken the body, grave clothes and all.

   a. John recounts that he "saw and believed." What do you think he "believed"?

   b. What, at this point, did John and the other disciples still not understand?

   c. How do you think John, as an old man living in Ephesus, was affected emotionally as he retold this story?

4. John's gospel ends in Galilee, where John himself was from. Read John 21:1–14.

   The Sea of Tiberias (v. 1) was likely the official Roman name for the Sea of Galilee. This name came from the town of Tiberias, which was named after the Roman emperor Tiberius Caesar. John and his brother James were the "sons of Zebedee" (v. 2). These six disciples didn't realize at first that this was the resurrected Jesus. This phenomenon

happened other times (e.g., John 20:14); Jesus either looked different or God prevented His followers from recognizing Him.

a. How do you think John, "the disciple whom Jesus loved" (v. 7), realized that this was Jesus?

b. What is the significance of the fact, as Michael notes, that rather than being accompanied by angels and glory, Jesus is there to make breakfast for His disciples?

5. **Finally, let's look at the last story in John's gospel. Read John 21:15–25.**

a. Why do you think Jesus told Peter that he would eventually have to follow Jesus to his own cross?

b. Do you agree with Michael that Peter, in verses 20–21, was actually showing concern for John, his "younger brother"?

DAYLIGHT ON PRAYER

A Time to Share

1. What have you appreciated the most about this study of the life of Jesus from the perspective of the gospel written by Jesus' friend John? How has this study sparked a yearning within you to "Come and see" more about Jesus?

2. As you look ahead in your spiritual journey, how can the group support you in prayer?

3. Michael Card states, in regard to Jesus' appearance to six of His disciples at the Sea of Galilee, "The fact that He's there serving His disciples, the fact that He's fixed a fire, He's cooked fish with those ruined hands, makes us want to fall down and worship Him more than if He had been there with angels and glory. And that's the consistent image in the gospel of John: Jesus the Servant-Lord."

    Conclude your time together by offering to Christ, our Servant-Lord, prayers of worship and commitment.